your in haste,
xx Kelsey
day

the Last four YeARS
Kelsey dAy

Chapter One: Growing Backwards

*this is where we start.
the worst moments
the ugliest parts of me.
welcome
and please
don't be afraid*

*"ink clung to your contrasts
but
all it did
in giving your edges darkness
was amplify the radiance
of you, Love."*
                    —siena ritter

earth fever

am i wasting this?
i plunged a thermometer into the backyard,
and the earth has a fever.
dosed in hallucinations
sweating and twisting beneath my shoes
the earth has a fever
but i go back to bed.
am i wasting this?
i wake up and plunge
white fencing into the backyard
the earth has a fever
but i dress in dark colors.
i've been told i would look good
in suits and oil bathtubs.
i plant myself in pavement and
turn my tie-dye into tapestries
for someone else to study.
am i wasting this?
the earth has a fever,
but i go back to bed.
the news clambers across pulsing headlines.
the grass shrieks sickly laughter
against smoky rain kisses
but still
i sleep
and drink out of a plastic bottle.
the earth has a fever
but i'm no doctor
anyway

therapy

sour mint
shedding skin
i stuff crinkled
leaves into your knuckles
then collapse and beg
for a diagnosis
i miss secret wednesdays
and leather chairs
where i sat with a spine
of light
crackling over my
kneecaps
waving my palm back
and forth beneath
the yellow as i spoke
portable sunshine
i risked taking

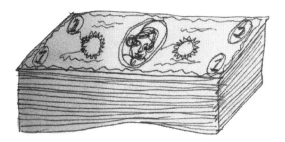

dontyoumind

swinging brown eyes
i've been thinking bout
freezing parking lots and
places beneath my feet
don't you mind
apologies always
dangling at my lips
i've been thinking bout
itching ankles and
taller buildings
don't you mind
from me to you
i've been thinking bout
leaving again
don't you mind

selective silence

what a sorry misfire of a person.
when i hear the screech of an ambulance
i open my journal and turn my music up.
ignorance
is an acquaintance i only speak with
when it's convenient.
selective silence
is such a villain
but tastes good
when i decide to swallow.
haunted hypocrite
what a horrible
holy
hypothesis

band-aid miles

the ear buds swung around my wrist,
snarling snakes scared to touch the ground
catching between my thumb and forefinger.
they hissed the cracked joints of a love song.
the wind smiled against my neck
i felt its teeth
i stood with
cloudy red shoes poised at the edge
i gazed down
swallowed the nauseating height
wondered what others saw when they looked down
wondered if it was normal to ache for the falling.
i thought about band-aids
and how many i would have to tape to the ground in a
straight line
before it would reach you
and i thought
even then
there couldn't be enough of them
to cover the chasms
beneath
my eyelids

comfortable nothing

neutral numb
horizons snap together
edges unreeling
these uneven curtains
are stuck in place
sweep me aside
and bury the left-overs
it's nothing specific
but i always feel this way
at night.

lonely

the blanket soaked into the mold of my skin
and scattered me into warm golden pieces of a girl
who was floating in tinfoil and ungiven kisses

3 am on a tuesday

what is this feeling?
lights off
lying on my back, eyes on the ceiling
enveloped in this
what,
what,
what is this feeling?
the walls in a cold sweat
figures grinning hazy
at the edge of my bed
i ignore it and rearrange my earbuds.
music up
lights off
but why?
i collected every clock in the house
and listened to their ticking,
everything erratic and out of sync,
i couldn't take it,
i buried them in the back yard
but why?
i smashed all the light bulbs
and wrote a poem in the pearly glass
my fingers haven't healed yet
3 am on a tuesday
music up, voices down, but why?
dusty floors kiss my feet
children smile and offer me burnt out matches
the microwave is broken
the clocks are broken
the lights are broken
the night is broken
maybe i'm broken.
12:41 am on a wednesday
my phone's stuck in a foreign language
music up, voices down
lights off,
don't listen to them,
and ignore this feeling like someone's

watching you through the window,
like there's someone there who wants you to
open the door for them
open the door for them
open the door and let in
a little more of them
no
no, music up, higher, voices down, lower,
push them out and ignore the unreal
but why?
the walls cackle with beads of sweat on their mouths
they say i shouldn't be so afraid
this is a chance to smile again
but why?
music up, voices down,
but what's the point?
open the door
no
music up, voices down
music up, voices down
no
but why?
i can hear the clocks in the backyard,
digging themselves out of their graves,
clawing through my window
tick tick tick
and suddenly it's 4:24 am on a thursday
open the door
but why
and the shattered light bulbs spell out a message i'm afraid to read
eyes shut
music up
nothing changes
i see buzzing light in sewer grates
i see dandelions collapsing into ashes
i see hair stuck to scissor blades
scissor blades stuck to shoulder blades
open the door

the music's not loud enough
but why?
8:54 am on a tuesday and
i found insect legs stuck to my ankles
i found broken fingernails in my pockets
someone asked me why and i kissed them on the mouth
voices up, music down
hand on the doorknob
but why?
i glued the broken light bulbs onto my wall
and arranged every resurrected clock into a circle around my bed
voices up, music down
tick tick tick
and it's 3:24 am on a monday
all i can smell is skin and wet paint
i can't remember what my name was
or what your name was
or why i ever fought this
so now i've named you sorry,
and start every sentence by addressing you
but why?
i've opened the door.
no.
voices up, music gone
no
i've opened the door
no
eyes flutter shut
and it's 3 am on a tuesday.
3 am on a tuesday, and the
earbuds have tied a noose around my neck
but i'm not gone yet.
i'm not gone yet
i'm standing in the doorframe
i'm standing
at the end
looking down
and i know now
i know

that there's only one thing left to do:
take the next step forward.
but why?

hello to something

awash in green
i feel it creeping:
a sick head rush
a tugging tangle
a compulsion
towards romance.
what use could i make
out of this

something's wrong with me

these red eyes seep into white walls
and i am hanging
loose and alone
from a ceiling fan.
when i close my eyes
i can flip the ground and dangle
like a puppet swooping from fraying strings.
my feet feel no loyalty to the ground
anymore.
and the pages don't
daydream about my thumbs
anymore
and my knees don't lock me upright
anymore
because i think they would all
rather be sleeping
i'm trying to conduct
some unstable imagery
but these words long for the ordinary
just as my pen rejects it
these throwaway moments
minor misfires
are what
paint me
green.

on the ragged edge of sleep

i twist the ring again and again
over the ridge on my finger.
memories leak from a tea bag
(swallow in silence)
then my drawstring lips pull tight.
sleep presses its hands against my neck.
feels for a pulse.
butterfly eyelids abandon flight
(they harbor such fear of migration)
wings stuck together,
sleep tightens around my neck
the light falls limp
and finally
it's quiet.

forecast

the world's waiting on snow again
and i think we're all just getting really good at
living in expectation
aching for the searing snow cast
we were promised
before the trees fought
for a final
breath

untitled

shark fins and trap doors
a noose disguised as a tie
or maybe a tie disguised as a noose
it's hard to tell with you
apple juice lips and skeleton slow dances
shaking the rain off our necks
a dying tree that holds our names
dying bodies who the names belong to
bruised tuesdays and empty afternoons
i say the same thing over and over again
in the hopes that sometime someone will listen
rusty knees and flooded dreams
i wont look too close because that's how you
make the wrinkles grow
a dropping iq and a war against oxygen
i can make flowers grow from your skin
i can write you an anthem
but i cant function quadratic equations so who the hell cares
turn my teeth to matches and my tongue to a cigarette
because every time i speak, my insides grow darker
"you've seemed so out of it lately"
maybe im just making things up
or maybe im stuck in a dream again
it all feels the same
they strapped a monitor to my chest and
my sister called me iron man
i used to not sleep at all
now i cant get out of bed
sometimes i want you to make assumptions
just not the wrong ones
im selfish like that
and sometimes i want to live
just not in the wrong way
and there seems to be so much wrong with these
faded walls and these faded people,
faded eyes, faded lies, cries, sighs
we're origami people, folding in on ourselves
im sorry

muddy shoes and red driveways
we're living a formula
copy and paste paper people into blank page lives
the ocean is so far away.
frozen feet and shipwrecked eyes
it's so hard to listen when my mind is telling me a story
i can't say out loud
"you seem distracted"
my mind is infested with scribbles
it's a wreck of tangled voices and it takes too long to
separate and unwind them
im sorry i didnt laugh at your joke
and that im always two steps behind you
when i used to be two steps ahead
but these days i can hardly hear you
through the weeds growing in my ears
im sorry
i swear i have good intentions
i want to write about the things that matter
but it always comes back to this
im sorry
possessed pencils and drifting interests
ive been sleeping too much
to be thinking this much about sleeping
they told me i had to talk to someone and
the voices took that as an invitation
i dont want to turn out the lights again
please
i dont want to see the stars again
i dont want to fall asleep again
dont you understand
i might not wake up this time
don't you understand
im too small im too nothing im too everything and
it's too much but not enough
im a speck of nothing, swallowed by the distance
im nothing im no one and someday the nothing will swallow
me whole
please no

please not tonight
dont hit the switch
dont tell the voices im awake
let me be
dont pull the light away from me,
dont pull it off my skin,
not yet,
please,
please
please
im sorry

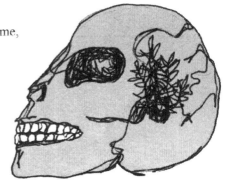

the song that played in the grocery store

we ventured down foreign aisles of milk and canned cookies
we drove there in a car that wasn't ours
and a song from america was playing.
i wanted to talk about everything back then
spit blood into your folded fists
pinch your ears open and use them as garbage disposals
now i count the syllables it takes to lie to you
swallow blisters, wear a hole in my throat
i get the groceries myself
or i stay in the car.

i won't be the first to speak

the lines of stitches
are ready to tug together
but my fingers pinch
and hold them apart
while
the sky picks at scabs
and the bed resists remaking
we're all so
terribly afraid
of healing

behind

what whispers have i left
in unspent places
how many words have i cradled
in undeserving eardrums
how many times
have i confessed
an accidental love?

year sixteen

and i'm sick of
sleeping on a gum-paper pillowcase
scraping sparks into your road-puddle eyes
and i'm sick of
thinking about seagulls when it's snowing outside
feeling nauseous with the barriers
and i'm sick of
rotted pumpkins and cold cider
holding you awake with hollowed arms
and i'm sick of
this
and i'm sick of
us
and i'm sick of
you

concealer

you write about the way
your skin craves the company
of blues and grays
squint at white lines
like they could point you in the right direction
your fingernails grow brittle
concrete highways stretching off skin
you write about the way
you love to leave scratch marks
on the ground
on the wallpaper
on the places you visit
footprints with a personality
but handshakes are such a bother.

bootprints

i do not like the feeling
of drinking apple juice from a coffee cup.
i do not belong here
squeezed between selfless people.
they're all advil and blankets
while i'm all fever and railings
i wish
i did more
to be like them.
i wish
i could file myself into a flood
and fill up this building
to make up for all the times
i didn't cry
but should have
to make up for all the times
i only cared
when i was obligated to.
i'm sitting here on an unstable wall
red and icy feet dangling
fifteen feet above a cracked parking lot
i'm remembering a little girl in orange lipstick
who clung to my elbow in public places
and i'm remembering boot prints in a parking lot
6 sets going in, 5 going out
i'm imagining her boot prints stamped somewhere in utah
while i'm sitting here
drinking apple juice out of a coffee cup

insomnia

darkness has never felt
so inviting

what college leaves behind

empty easter-egg house
in a frayed basket neighborhood
i try not to look
because now reeks of next
these days.
my brother breathes pavement dust
somewhere in south carolina
he salutes to slumber
and reads of backwards places.
my best friend breathes numbers
in a building i've never seen before
he visits in the hazel sleep of summer
but i can walk nowhere
without stepping on a piece of him.
my father has turned to a ghost town
hollow bones, haunted eyes howling
to press rewind
my mother mixes hot chocolate into her coffee
even though she prefers the bitter taste
everything inverts in the emptiness.
so now i sit still enough
to hear sand pass through an hourglass.
now i sit still enough
to feel this neighborhood drying out
to feel this childhood
drying out
now i sit still enough
to starve in the left behind
now i sit still enough
to anticipate
the finish line.

sunless

i don't miss the sun.
not
like i used to

the beach

there i was
passenger seat soaked blue and
mom's hand on the radio
i couldn't drive then.
or pull my sleeves up when i sweated
or kiss without leaving myself behind
two days away
i was
dreading my father's face
missing a boardwalk boy with my
entire empty casing
i offered up my insides
handed this place a fistful of entrails
left there a musty muted me, in sand and
a tourist trap late night abandoned
i'll never see again.
the swimming pool
dimmed and lazy lone lights
met me at the witching hour
aliens slept in the hotel
my mother among them
then there i was
passenger seat soaked blue
seeping blurry slight light
swallowing salt and sand
infected with the nighttime
never
never again

oops

i ignored the sunken signs
and found the swimming pool
i sank into the sound of suffocation
wavered weightless, climbed to the bottom
felt the breathless water close in
the layers of silence pressed down
and i savored the crushing closeness
this was familiar
this was like being held
but closer.

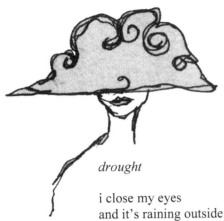

drought

i close my eyes
and it's raining outside
i swear
i can feel it from here
i can feel the
sidewalk chalk loosen its grip,
i can feel the
gasp of grateful restful earth
i can feel the
windows sagging with a soggy sigh.
i close my eyes
and it's raining outside.
the doors are closed.
the walls are tingling. but
i swear
i can feel it from here.
when they lead me outside,
sun falls from a blank sky
dry light, helpless
the grass wails for water
a wasteland unwet
but i close my eyes
and it's raining outside.
it's raining outside.
i swear

rehearsing remedy

i've locked all my bones in place
and i've memorized
these ear-kissing arguments
rehearsing remedy
like that'll draw it
closer.
did i summon this sickness?
you take the puppet's place
and we kiss with
lips tugging on strings
maybe i never should have
started this
on that threading dark-eyed night
maybe i just
adopted regret
as my pastime
my body
never provided
for this.
this.
my breath and my blood.
my dna, left
in a sidewalk.

seatbelt

we pulled into the cracked white lines
and saw you in the next car over
a cigarette flapping out your lips.
smoke snaked between your teeth
slithered through our window
and tied a knot around the boy sitting behind me
the boy in the baby seat
the one we keep trying to protect
the one with the new pajamas
your son
and i'm supposed to be the kind one but
that day the road tilted beneath my feet
and i'm supposed to be the writer but
the words collapsed inside me
my father told him it was time to go see mommy
and kelsey will unbuckle you and then we'll go
and i just stared at that little kid
and he just stared back
and my dad said it again
and i just stared at that little kid
and he just stared back
and you smoked in the next car over
and i thought maybe if i didn't unbuckle him he wouldn't
have to go
and that little kid's eyes seemed to flicker
and i wondered what he was thinking
and i just stared at that little kid
and he just stared back
and my dad leaned over
and he clicked the buckle

i don't know what else to say

my spine
is the only thing
holding me up
today

these sorts of seasons

the open night
invades our skin
some seasick punishment
of home.
how can we defend ourselves
against these sorts of seasons?
i could lure
sinew and servants
late-footed in the looking
i could litter what's left
lie
in the voice of a nightingale.

giving (away)

silk ribbons nestle into eyelids
bows blossom around my throat
hold down, hold tight
how to brace
against giving yourself away
i fold my clothes
into perfect squares
of gift wrapping
tuck in the corners of my bed sheets
with packing tape
snap my spine in half
bend my neck to my toes
slide my skin into an envelope
i pack myself into a cardboard box
frame my bones in pale pink tissue paper
and when i'm done
being passed around
maybe i'll find refuge
in the dusty corner
of an attic

vice

i'm still secretly hoping
that god
has found a way
to miss me

CHApTeR TWO: HiM

in which all my love poems,
"love" poems,
and poems about love
exist in the same place.
welcome
and please
remember that i am still learning

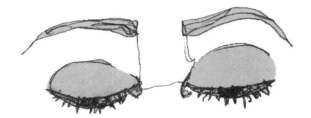

*"the leaves are losing themselves for the sake of the trees
but just for a moment,
they get to fall."*

—holly greene

places to know you

i want to see you in the white light of a gas station
when the space outside us is dripping summer nighttime
i want to see you surrounded by other heartbeats
wrapped like a jacket around the spine of someone else
i want the orange peels on your floor
and the pencil shavings at the bottom of your book bag
i want to see you crack your knuckles
force a smile and raise your eyebrows
i want the computer code racing behind your eyes
and the clumsy curl of your lips
when i look up
and say
good morning.

goodnight

it's been three months
of reaching to remember reasons
we wanted this.
three months of
tasting different accents and
practicing how to miss each other and
saying goodnight across time zones –
what a relentless routine
we've made out of this.
what a
subtle surrender
we've made
to the distance

unattached, we ran

unattached, we ran.
i left my shoes in the car.
a muffled ruffled boy
with in-between eyes
stood there wearing your clothes
always so cool
slipping my car keys into his pocket
he warned me
of cracked bottles and gravel,
so i let him
carry me through a playground
as he invented new ways
to kiss me.
he's new to this
reaching for skin
hungry for wet paint lips
i marked myself all over in sky blue tape
then let our fingers touch
unattached, we ran.
clumsy birds
galloping under polluted skylight
peeking through
dark library doors.
our first home was here
and we discover again
concrete clouds
the night
envies us
for the way
we crawl
towards the light
and i guess
i'll miss you
in the morning.

my local library in terms of lost lovers

my library is the place where thoughts
grow branches, grow wings
my library is the place where most things
become possible things
i have loved in this place where
clock hands tremble with the weight
of an abstract concept
i have loved in different places of this place
and here is the run-down:

one.
the tree on the far corner of the wilting lawn
is where i lay beside my first love.
the first love that i loved,
this is where i
looked at the sky between cracks in the branches,
the triangles between tree fingertips,
it is where i delivered my best and worst apology.
it is where i kissed you, as autumn lost its breath.
we were cut from a bad movie
we carved our names into the bark and that was
the first sign of what was wrong with us:
why did we equate violence with permanence?
why did you carry a blade in your pocket,
like you were just waiting for me to ask?
who were we, to mutilate a tree for the sake
of feigning romance?
why did we prove ourselves
by forcing ourselves into something else?
our names don't belong there.
our names don't belong there.

two.
the secret room in the back of the library.
this wasn't my first love per-say, perhaps
my first half-love, my
love before love, yes, i was
entranced by the distance of you.

i matched your laugh to a text ding,
got annoyed when you said the word sex –
i should be clear
it was *eighth grade* and
our hands never touched.
i was fascinated by your flannel shirts untucked,
socks black and rolled way up up
we were both writers and had a flare for theatrics
so you can imagine just how well we both ended up.
we spent countless november evenings alight in night
searching for the right word
as wind slammed into the library's sightless windows.
i watched the way you typed like
a bird sat on the corner of your wrist
and i smiled
when i thought
you weren't looking.

three.
the blue-lit parking lot, where i
stood barefoot and empty before you
shivering
beneath angled rooftops.
i was a pale expectation reaching for a dreamscape.
you were silent and
though you preached of nighttime
you never knew lonely.
i drove us everywhere
your phone always dead
your hands always still
your eyes always somewhere else,
you sat in the passenger seat
and looked out the window
looked in the mirror
looked anywhere but here
i would have died for a half glance.
for a flicker of yourself to reach for me.
for any movement
any attempt

to close the distance.
we ate at blue restaurants
you paid the bill but
wouldn't look at me still
we ran through a skeleton playground
our hands reached through gray wind
almost
we were never closer than then
what a winter love.
frozen lips, snowflake fingertips
alone
when you sat alongside me
when we stood
lonely
in the library parking lot
what a winter love.

remote

eyes change channels –
two television screens
screaming static
and i'm locked against a brick wall again
a flower between my teeth
the rooftop apologetic
when the rain stings our foreheads.
silence.
stillness.
a paused world,
stopping and restarting every time he draws near.
the sidewalk holds its breath when he speaks.
he makes this place just as nervous
as he makes me

unreceived messages

"i'm sorry."
"the plane is about to leave."
"i saw a poster that reminded me of you."
"i don't know when you'll get these messages."
"seeing the ocean made me think of you."
"do you believe in ghosts?"
"my poems are about you. all of them."
"and whenever i wonder, i am wondering about you."
"i wonder if you still have that dumb plastic pearl i gave you."
"you're the last thing i think about at night."
"i heard a song that reminded me of you."
"i wonder if you are going to be the same person when i come back."
"do you still care?"
"i wonder if you'll ever get these messages."
"i miss you."
"i wonder if you'll forget about me."
"i love you."
"sometimes i think i hear your voice."
"i love you."
"do you remember my name?"
"i love you."
"i remember yours. i remember everything."
"i love you."
"funny, isn't it, how after you say a word
for long enough, it begins to lose its meaning."
"i love you."
"is that what you did to my memory?"
"i love you."
"did you play it in your head once too many times?"
"i love you."
"please don't forget me."
"i love you."
"please."
...
...
"please."

synonymous

violets over his shoulder
and a knife in his pocket
i unlearned how to sleep
when i was with him
unlearned how to breathe.
we met in the softest shade of violence
slept in a bomb shelter when the sun was out
kissed with blood in our teeth.
call it love
call it ache
the words
are the same
now

sophomore something

is this what you wanted?
a scent like cinnamon and damp earth
your eyes infected with my image
your band aides in the garbage can
blurred sight and open sky
am i what you wanted?
don't forget our silent field
and the flowers i still can't stop stealing
pull down your hood and follow me
don't forget the picture your little sister drew me
five years old and proud of her new scented markers
your scribbled handwriting on the back, promising to love me
"the sky colored pen smells the best."
the taste of your half-truths and soft breath
messy hair and cold hands
i don't know why you ever chose me
sharp heat and red trees
i don't ever want to keep track of your bruises again
golden edges and curving darkness
every moment with you aches with nostalgia
blurring shapes and distant voices
please don't leave me now
numb eyes and desperate lips
don't leave me
empty halls and white walls
don't
don't
don't.

doors

the doors slam shut in his eyes
the locks grind into place
and i am left
shivering in the hallway
trying to live off the light that leaks out
from under
the doors

reunion

re-arrival and this is all
rust and dust, lust that must
mean something like
seeing you again.
laughter itches in my throat,
eyes flick up and away, up and away,
hesitation.
hands shaking, gazes drifting
my voice loses its way
when i try to pull away from you.
i can swing across this distance
watch you come closer
swallow the beehive in my throat
swallow the parasite thoughts
swallow the conversations you don't remember.
i'm good at this.
selective memory smiles
in the face of a reunion

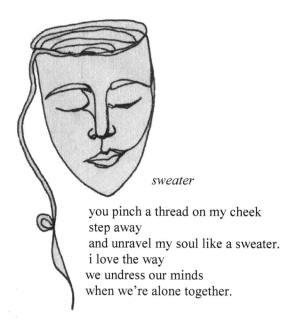

sweater

you pinch a thread on my cheek
step away
and unravel my soul like a sweater.
i love the way
we undress our minds
when we're alone together.

ash tray

i inhale
you
a quick fix turned to burnt lips
and i guess i've missed the taste
of sickness

you promised not to tell

waiting in a bright room
violets sprout from your kneecaps
flowers ripe with grief
a garden of blacks and blues
the petals sway in lilted laughter
as the roots push in
deeper
bent teeth
smashed fingernails
i wish i didn't know about the way
you drag your tongue
over the truth
i wish i didn't know
about the nights
you wrapped yourself in tinfoil
to keep warm
shaking thighs
cracking lips
my name, stuck in your throat
a confession, latched in your lungs
bite marks gleam on your knuckles
secretive slashes
and i was
supposed
to help you

after

i hope you can still taste
the laugh
i left
against your lips

planning

he built a plastic city to meet her in.
he coaxed a crowd onto the streets and showed off blueprints and formulas.
but she is not a house to be built one day.

your pieces in the passenger seat

i drove through
a mud ditch
to gather your pieces
in the passenger seat
imagined christmas lights
tangled in your hair
to light up your mind
just a little
and i never learned
to shut my mouth about you
forget to
open it about me
but we're just beginning
and i like it this way

but anyway

you rescued a hummingbird from a spiderweb
cupped its emerald softness in your hands
and tugged white film from its feathers
but anyway.
the sky is bleeding again
my feet fell in love with the sidewalk and
you asked me why i'm always barefooted
how strange, how unclean
the bottoms of my feet always want to
kiss the ground that holds them
i shrug my shoulders
but anyway.
teach my eyelids to miss one another
i microwave a cup just to
watch the steam unravel
you blink twice
and i'm re-learning morse code
i forget how we got here
but anyway.
my elbows dig into the table
i cross then uncross my legs
and you blink
twice, three times
a signal to speak
and for the first time
i almost do.
but anyway.

a song set in skull

accidental butterflies
don't unravel
you have a net for a ribcage
and a song set in skull
skin scraped love
i will
love it
or for it
i will love

colony

my stomach was not earth
to drive flags into
my lips were not plastic
to tape barcodes over
you have
a new scar on your cheek
i dream
of pressing my lips against
that healing line
but
my nightmares
are filled
with your
imperialistic fingertips

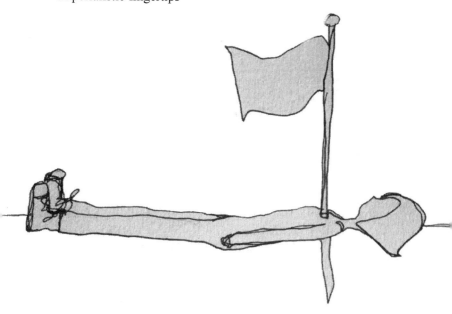

arms & away

i'm so wrapped up in
arms and away
and god i miss the
music of your eye light
maybe i love the way you
turn away
because it's only then
i want you
closer

bus door

late lights crawl over bedsides
and i hear the bus door hiss shut
at the edge of your driveway
how do i always end up
practicing eulogies and hiding silverware
you said you had nothing to lose
nothing to leave behind
i guess you didn't count me
i am ceilings and closets tonight
skin stuck to pavement
cold and low crawling tonight
i only wanted
a heartbeat

we shouldn't talk when we get like this

i'm so scared of this stunted sunlight
this flaring empathy, i am
recalling recovery
exactly where it met the methods.
let's respond and react
until we reach
and miss all over again
you scare me so much
when you talk like this –
again and again
it retakes the beast. and i can't.
anymore.
but i will not ask of the wild

deadly sunday

you know what the problem is?
you are far too familiar
with the places i used to pray to
constantly adjusting and adapting
for a crooked higher source
and i don't want to be
your worship.

take 2 in action

drop off
cold and awake
we switch cd's
and try again.
it's easiest to talk
when i can hold a drink
and watch ice seep clouds into coffee
i swish my straw round and round
hissing against the rim of the cup
blowing bubbles into laughter
looking anywhere but you.
night is out of breath now
it aches with every inhalation
seeking sleep
i wish i could wrap my arms around it
and say that it's safe with me
i forget you've been speaking
wish that the night was sleeping
or time would crawl away from me
we never got along
but i respect its decaying beauty

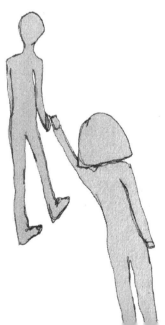

it's been a year and i'm still here

silk covers twist
under spine and elbows
teach my dreams
to silence
wilted memory
the hot chocolate burned
the inside of your mouth
chapped chalky lips
kissing in daylight
on television screens
you said we were alone
they took
our pictures
through car windows
they watched us
over newspaper and coffee
you said we were alone

lowercase

i awoke with
your hands gripped around my neck
in the dark met
two eyes so deep-set into sadness
and i swore i would never
scream
again
so i reached up
weak arms straining to stop
and i whispered it
because you
never listened
to capital letters
anyway

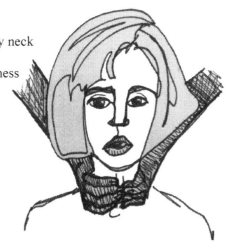

betrayal in the form of silence

i knew a bitter blue boy who spoke the language of the rain.
veins ran green beneath his fingernails. he was a gift of the
evening, a narcissistic gleam from the corner of a cracked
mirror
and he loved the snow just like every boy.
in his presence, i scarcely breathed.
my dreams had already spent so much time sighing at his
lightlessness. we argued about everything. we hid, anemic in
coffee shops when it was winter outside. and we sucked the
sun from each other.
i knew a bitter blue boy who spoke the language of the rain.
i thought he led me into unlit places, closets and exiles of
muted magic, but he was never leading me. i was merely
following. he had little interest in a girl wrapped in flowers,
trying to conjure the spring.
he was busy pressing lip and teeth into ice trays. he was
never one
for the springtime
anyway.
i knew a bitter blue boy who spoke the language of the rain.
but he only ever spoke
silence
with me

post

i won't
draw a list, a graph, a novelistic masterpiece
on ways you could have prolonged this.
that would be unfair to you
and i'm trying
to adjust to your face out of its usual context
so forgive me if i mourn you
from a distance.
fucked up friendless futures
never felt the oxygen
they never changed
colors
but that's just your culture, isn't it?
the kind that's silent.
the kind that would rather,
look away.

i confessed in my best friend's driveway

could i count the moments
i felt the push of you breathing
my cheek sunk into the hollow
of your shoulder
you,
my reminder of
clockhands and tomorrows
you,
my evasion
and homelight
you,
the definition of risk.
could i track the progressions
of dreams
where i visit you?
you,
the deepest height
and those hands i have memorized
the risk
is what makes it
worth it

stages of re-seeing

undone and redone
gray among your lying teeth
blue
stretching, sweeping
sweat
red like endings, paper cuts, closing throats
and shivering
everywhere
unable and turning off
restart
green
flying and crashing, breaking down
like every false landing that led me here
i can't
do this
yellow
deep, razor thin, open chest…
light-less

hall

we pass
despite our pledge
and our eyes feign unfamiliar.
we pass
and i reach up to
rustle my hair,
knuckle to forehead,
a subtle re-adjustment,
for the same reason
the wind sways a forest –
mostly
to remind passerby
that we never lost
ownership.

division

it's you, hello and
i am yet to feel sick to my stomach
thank god
i have become accustomed
to the mental math
of us
thank god
i have at last accepted
the division.
we pass
and we are nothing
but uneven leftovers
you gave less
so at least you have more
now that the problem
is over

hungry

we are
hazy half-bright
in a rain sore night
surrounded by skeptic outlines,
creeping for a camera flash.
we were
tourists in love
until we found our hometowns
in one another
we will be
bedrock clifftops
hands diving into rib gaps
shoveling in skull gardens
constantly
digging for more
of each other.

branches breaking

when we glimpse one another
i hear wind slamming against windows
and feel my chest like branches breaking –
it takes days for the color to come back.
i've held
these numbers between my shoulder blades
eyes molded shut as the digits
tick into the negatives
free falling
into old habits and indifference,
i wish you would
look up
every once in a while.

tangle

i forgot how to
write about me
without somehow
writing about you
too

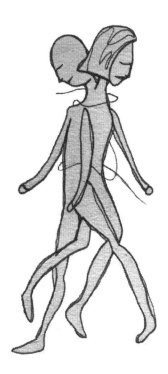

permission for reconstruction

let me stumble.
let me stretch and ache in your direction.
i like to give you my words
without you ever seeing them.
i like to make you
into something else
when no one but me
can see it.
you,
but mutated into something
real enough
for poetry

spelling words

i am held, fingernails to flesh
scraping and shaping and shaking
in your direction,
i am hooked up to the very edge
hanging onto your
absolute fucking soul
who knew i could
itch and strain
for something so familiar?
close my eyes
and guide my hands across your lips
when you speak
my fingers want to
taste the letters
of an i love you
pull me down and lift me apart
sort me into categories
the lilt of my voice
the color of my shoes
the sharp arc of my breath
combinations and rearrangements
to print on index cards
and memorize.
this is how we are now.
what a perfect end
to a rainy day.

old investments

i don't know what to make of these
unfamiliar elbows
a different stare reaching into a past i
haven't figured out yet
when will i recognize the curve of your thumb
and the shape of your kneecaps
and why do i taste him on the tips of your lips
i think there's a part of me
still invested
in the place i loved before you.
and i have to wonder
how much of myself i can invest now
without leaving fault lines
between you
and your better someone
i guess he will always
have
a part of me

i'm trying to be patient

it's silence, only empty yawning palms
and silence with nothing in between
it's only silence but
it's his silence
and i listen
because there's so much more
i'm hoping
he'll say

secret

i am starving
for a new kind
of thunder

define

i'm tangled in your connotations
aloof and alight
in your historic eyesight
our eyes will always be in love.

our eyes caught and i swear the world ended

where would you crease the covers
if i invited you into the bed of a conversation?
i'd watch a
lopsided body stretch to brush a memory
or a pillowcase
i could press into the vein we let drip rust candy
taste a cinnamon nightmare
and wake up bleeding sweat –
i regret you
in the micro pause when our souls recognize each other
in that
catastrophic glance across the classroom
and i think
despite everything
our eyes will always be in love.

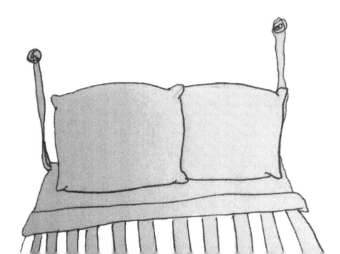

gentle

the whispering pop of
your lips on my hair
a breaking surface
a fight against parting
you don't know
how much
i shiver

perfume to meet you

i don't wear
a special perfume,
no greasy rose
wrist-breath
in preparation
to meet you.
what safety
is this

it doesn't matter anyway

i wonder what you think of this skepticism.
me, an adjoinment between steamed windows and broken
eyesight
good at kissing and
just damaged enough
i wonder what you think of this skepticism.

i'm trying to understand you

i've never known
a kiss
so unselfish

sip

cradle me like a wineglass between your fingertips
sip from my secrets
slide your tongue across the edge of the glass
and risk
a taste of this darkness

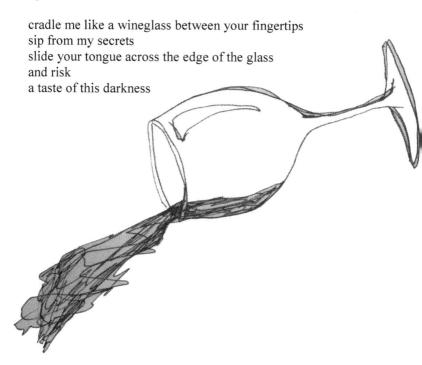

affirmation

i do not know much but i do know this:
something in me
aches for you.

Chapter Three: ME

sleeping, breathing, being
here i am
in every complexity
welcome
and please
let a little light in

"i think i spend too much of my time turning myself into a concept.

like, i make myself into this artistic entity – the tall girl with the short hair and dark eyes, the one who carries a journal and wears black, the girl with secrets and a loud laugh. someone worth loving. someone who wants to be loved.

and yes, maybe the concept of me wants to be in love. but it would be so much easier to just be a concept, not a human being who has to actually feel and breathe and exist and experience and experiment and face loving. if i were no more than a concept, then at least i could face love on equal terms. instead i am a real creature, trapped in skin and bone and physicality, and i am at the mercy of an unreachable abstract concept.

i am not a character in a book, i am not an idea, i am a human being.

what a gift. and what a terror, to behold."

– me

i am

i am:
anything but rest,
unsilence and reliving.
i am:
unresolved and retrying,
alive and leaking luckful life.
i am:
bloodless smears of color,
pulsing between fingers.
i am:
a selfish attempt
at dreaming backwards.
always hungry
and reaching

where

senseless me,
somewhere
in the midst of
everything
that bleeds

isn't that what you wanted

pin me down
to the hungry carpet
crush down my shoulders and
file every jutting angle
into the sugar softness
you wish for.
press my voice into a whisper
my tuesday nights into sunday mornings
undo and redo
everything lethal about me.
i think
maybe then
i could
miss her

seven ways to look at the sky

one.
you lay sprawled across the earth,
breathing in sync with the dirt you rose from.
fingers tangled in grass, a sweet green romance,
you squint against the sun and
let the sky reach down to meet you.

two.
your eyes swing from a scarline school desk
to remember the skyline.
it feels illegal to look out the window here.
you have work to do.
a dull pencil and a calculator that's out of battery.
but still, for just a moment,
you allow yourself to look.
and see.

three.
through the windshield,
above that white toyota's sunroof.
stuck in traffic, you
are what the sun waits for.

four.
in the night,
you stand barefoot and
let the night taste you.
let the clouds sink down and
whisper under your jawline.
it's too hazy to see the night's skin.
but the clouds are so alive.

five.
unalone.
you drive out onto the parkway
with a group of people who have seen you cry.
you wrap your arms around each other,
sink into the mountains,

merge into the same something.
and you look up, transfixed, unfixed.

six.
a half-glance over your shoulder,
easily forgotten
then.

seven.
standing at the side of the road
knees bent,
shoulders sloped,
a sweater pulled down over your elbows.
you have never felt so unreal.
nothing matters anymore.
but there is light
above you.

the fourth of july

cross-legged on the pavement
in the dewy night heat of summer,
fingers trace chalk drawings.
i feel underwater here.
we ride our bikes together in thrumming summer darkness
voices bounce off the road and into the trees, and
the chalk clouds still ache
with the color

hello

i arrived, alive
with all these
unsilent struggles

winter

i've only ever fallen in love
when it was cold out

i ran into depression at the grocery store

oh my god hi!
how are you, wow it's been so long
sorry, i know, i've just been so *busy*
i've been practicing unreality
just like you taught me
wow, i thought you were gone for good
wow, no, really, it's – it's so good to see you!
i – yeah!
no, really, i've just, i've just been
busy
so busy
you hug just like you used to,
you know that?
ribs touching ribs
have you lost weight?
no, i haven't been seeing anyone else, but
for the record it's really none of your – what?
no.
well, see
i'd love to catch up
really, i would
it's just that i
i've just
i've been so
busy
i just came here to get some eggs
i really don't have much time to talk
i should really get going
another hug?
you smell like mint gum and cheerios.
no, i'm not saying it's a bad thing, it's just
listen
i should really go
i left the car running
i know
listen
it was good catching up

no, not any time soon
i'm really just
terribly busy at the moment
no,
i don't need you to walk me out to the car
i think i've got it
no, really,
but thank you
i really wasn't expecting to run into you today
let's just hold out
and
all right
i guess i'll see you
first thing
in the morning

well, i

i am a hodgepodge of placement.
what am i but
something that sinks?
something that drifts? uncertain?
what am i but an
ordinary moment?
gone and new as soon as it happens?
i am a hodgepodge of placement.

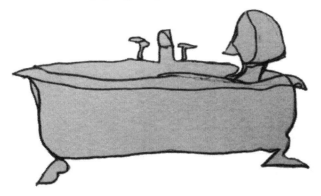

a sisterhood to streetlight

i felt a loyalty to the lights we drove by.
connected somehow
i imagined
a labyrinth of luminous lights
unspooling from my middle
racing across the road to kiss streetlamps
i felt a sort of sisterhood with them.
a responsibility
attached by glowing cords
to the glowing signs
and blinking stoplights
bleeding worry
into windshields.

tall girl

my body knows better than me
that there are higher places i can reach.
why else
would my kneecaps reach the skyline
my feet invisible so far below me
too often i begged gravity to give me a little extra
when i should have
kissed the sky's blue skin
while
i was up there

crash

i was held there in traffic cone clatter
detaching and re-assembling
then asleep with
my nose pressed to a cinnamon pillow.
my father likes to say you should get
seven hours of sleep at night.
i don't drive anymore
my foot was always numb on the pedal
someone adjusted the mirrors and
i broke the windshield
but at least
i avoided
the bigger collision
i don't drive now
the cinnamon music is always too loud
my hand is splintered
down the knuckles
my skin still breathes
glass powder
i don't drive anymore
but at least
i am avoiding
the bigger collision
so now there's
never a chance
of closing my eyes on cruise control
and
no one can take the wheel from me
when i sit in the passenger's seat
at least i will never
catch a glimpse of
cinnamon eyes
in the rearview mirror
i give up control to be in control
but at least
i am avoiding
the bigger collision.

invasion

up.
and there's that. feeling.
GAY.
three, four.
GAY, AND
YOU'RE GOING TO DIE TOMORROW.
one.
one, two, three. up now. **GAY.** three, four.
this is an intrusive thought. **YOU ARE GOING TO DIE TOMORROW.**
let it go.
let it go. three, four. one, two, three, four.
two feet on the floor
and there's that. feeling.
YOU'RE GOING TO FAIL.
this is an intrusive thought.
AM I GAY?
three, four. this is an intrusive thought. three, four.
YOU'RE GOING TO DIE TOMORROW.
let it go. you need to do your school work. this is an intrusive thought?
I'M GAY.
let it go.
YOU USED TO LIKE TO READ. YOU DON'T HAVE TIME TO READ ANYMORE.
YOU'RE NEVER GOING TO ACCOMPLISH YOUR DREAMS.
teeth clenched against teeth. hands sweating, shaking. three. four.
WHY ARE YOU EVEN TRYING?
three, four. this is an intrusive thought.
YOU USED TO LIKE BEING ALONE.
YOU'RE GOING TO DIE TOMORROW.
this is an intrusive thought.
IF YOU DON'T DIE TODAY, IT'LL BE TOMORROW. IF NOT TOMORROW, THE NEXT DAY.

stop. this is an intrusive thought.
let it go.
please,
let it go. three, four.
i'm
trying.
NOT
GOOD ENOUGH.
where do we go. from here.
GAY.
three, four.
DIE TOMORROW.
i'm
glitching,
half thoughts
freezing,
fracturing.
this is an intrusive
please. please, just
do not
feed into
BUT YOU'RE GOING TO DIE TOMORROW
hospital beds and gravestones
do not
but now i'm
googling symptoms
tapping
three, four.
one, two, three
one, two, three, four, please
this is an intrusive
YOU'RE GOING TO DIE TOMORROW
stop
three, four
and there's that. feeling.
YOU'RE NOT A GOOD PERSON
AND NO ONE LIKES YOU
these thoughts keep coming they've
got to mean
something

don't they?
stop
this is an intrusive
please
AM I GAY?
stop it
this is pointless
YOU'RE GOING TO DIE TOMORROW
YOU'RE GOING TO DIE TOMORROW
three, four.
three, four.
three.
three.
three.
three.
three.
three.
.
.
.
four.

swimming in december

i look for
the wild
in freezing
p l a c e s
find
the wild
in torrents
of ice
and collision

a place where
god
breathed
once

a virtue

i am not patient.
time is always
pressing laughter against me
i can always hear it breathing
i am not patient.
i do not wish to watch the clock hands
draw circles around the issues we're ignoring
no
i am not patient.
i am implosion.
i am running.
i am heaving lungs and burnt tongues and i will not
slow down
for you

i have something to say

my voice is chasing me out doorsteps
flying behind corners
leaving me somewhere
searching

if not someone

are we not all of the same place?
the first cell?
the first same something?
i've been dreaming of kisses lately.
i've been dreaming of skin, spines,
the place where one edge meets another.
why do i exist, if not to love.
why do i exist, if not to reach for the borders.
are we owed anything in living.
is to be born to be deserving of something?
be deserving of everything?
what am i, if not undeserving.
what am i, if not alive, if not dying, if not wanting,
learning, hurting, healing.
what is this feeling, like suffocation from the inside.
what am i, if not a poet.
if not a someone, who bleeds.
if not a someone, who dreams.
i'm trying to listen.
i swear.

concert

were you an exit sign?
i feel like i've entered a different dimension
dress to undress
my wrists like broken necks
i'm the type of person who talks in movie theatres.
tell me how i can bow in the right direction,
navy flames through my teeth
i've been told not to fight a war of mimickery
kissing elbows
i didn't see you there
let it go?
fine.
bring on the cold.

introductions

i know we've just met, but i've gotta ask.
are you the type to…unreach for people?
to slide skeletal hands into pockets.
to…unsmile, when i look at you.
i know we've just met, but
how loud do you talk?
does your voice like the sound of itself speaking?
do you ever…misspell words, on purpose?
are the type to undraw portraits just to
re-see the beginning of things
do you ever
rise in love?
and by rise in love i mean, do you ever
fall in love backwards? well i
guess what i'm trying to ask is
do you see opportunity when you look at me?
do you see… me, when you look at me?
what do you think about harry potter?
do the movies make you feel old inside?
are you the type to feel old inside?
do you ever set your watch a few minutes ahead
to make sure that you won't be late?
are you constantly in search of unstolen imagery
trapped in tunes unoriginal
wrap the sky like a shawl around your shoulders
what do you think about questions?
do defined endings make it easier.
blank statements marching across conversation
how does it feel to loop a question mark
around the corner of your lips?
i'm sorry. i know we just met. my name is kelsey
i wanna be a writer
i'm 17
i'm from boone, north carolina
and i'm sorry:
i was just
wondering.

purpose

i was born to tiptoe
into mahogany secrets
to hide in the buttery breath between "betters"
to look across brick buildings
in search of definition
i was born to be a witness.
i was born to love -- though not, perhaps
to love you,
still,
to love
to miss the mountains
while they wait for me.
i was born to reach
reach for stoplights
reach for pens
reach for curtains
to stand alongside a highway
that sings like a seaside
i was born to cram headaches into jam jars.
i was born to swirl smiles into tea
and offer you a sip
when the walls
burn green.

systematic undoing

i have a system of ropes under my skin
strange contraption
my veins carriers of an unsewn project
pinch a vein
loop my arteries into a frilly bow
wrap me into a gift
pinch a vein
and tug
but wait
to unravel

no

you are a soldier of love.
a mechanism, caught in the act of change
you'd like to be smaller, easier to kiss, is that
the point of you?
voices realign
and you find yourself silent
again

it's raining in my hometown today

it's raining in my hometown today.
there, it is a darker shade of magic.
i imagine the trees, humming to the
lilt of the air, the wind stumbling over
crackling edges.
i imagine chimneys and hickories
skeletons cackling on front porches
tea in sweaty glasses
and roadsides.
it's raining in my hometown today.
this is good for the tomato plants.
for the dusty boulders and
tin roofs and
backyard black bears and
the mountains.
it's raining in my hometown today.
and it is without me, today,
to mourn
to miss.
it is raining in my hometown today.
perhaps it cries
with the missing of me.

something like inspiration

i miss lying paralyzed
overtaken in creation
attacked and attached
glass eyes spinning kaleidoscope spirals
who turned out the lights

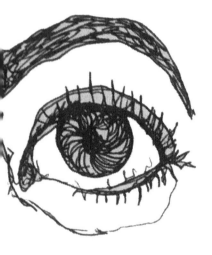

of boston

red shoes on black granite
i'm sunk in a yellow couch
breathing mint and lysol.
is the city light leaking through the walls?
i wish there was a window here i could open
a way i could tell the night
that it's welcome here.

everywhere i step
roots sprout from my heels
trying to dive into the sidewalk and take hold
trying to keep me here
maybe one day i'll come back
and slow down enough
to let my feet plant themselves a home

but 'til then i'll walk on my tiptoes
and i'll stretch when i walk by the skyscrapers
a place like this makes a tall girl feel at home

hand me a jacket and tube of toothpaste
temporary tastes gray in my mouth
hand me a smile and a roomkey
i need a membership to clarity

white hands on a yellow couch
paint, black and empty
is the city light leaking through the walls?

it's late and we're driving and all i can think is

1. the moon is hazy under plastic wrapping.
   i swear i saw a figure waving at the edge of the road

2. he sits
   eyes closed with his arm out the window.

3. is this what home is?
   a distortion of affection
   consumed by collective concerns
   brought back again
   to winter dresses and smothered edges.

4. he leans between the wind and window
   challenging early exit signs
   rolling over yellow lines and parental murmurs.

5. i've come to crave these criticisms.
   i've come to miss
   sighing
   and lying
   with the li[e]ghts off
   shaky letters shivering under timelines
   driving just to drive
   writing because i am still living,
   reimagining my beginnings.

6. she always loved this song
   and i love the shape of her hands.
   i watch the way she holds the steering wheel
   scrolls the volume up a little
   so the walls of this metal machine
   rattle with rhyming rhythm.

7. for just an instant
   i'm nine years old again
   and feel invisible strings from me to the moon...
   as though i am my own gravity
   as though i am something to be followed.

8. what strange and sorry thoughts i have
   in the nighttime.

9. i'm glad i'm not dead
   but it's complicated
   it's more complicated than that
   a strain for simplicity
   it's dark there
   but i'm a friend of the nighttime

10. i'm tired
    so tired
    my brain tells me all the wrong things
    why not analyze these anagrams?
    compile the complaints and explain
    what is it that makes me so unhuman.

11. i guess i just
    like the act of
    leaving

a solution to the silence

here i am
dropping question marks
over every establishment of authority
driving barefoot
as my windshield heaves freezing
here i am
an experiment in the act of being
a hypothesis in the act of becoming
here i am
labeling layers of growth
dancing across lined pages and
erasing knuckle-led love songs
here i am
a solution
to the silence

so why not

the tree
doesn't choose
to grow

when you will grow

one.
alone on the beach.
you will sneak out two minutes past twelve
and follow your feet to the sand domes.
you will hold your arms out in front of you
admire the invisibility
taste the salty darkness
and feel the sky, as it settles into your scars.
the stars will pry your scars open,
to let the light out.

two.
eight years old, in the shower.
you will stare at your kneecaps,
at how the water carves veins
across the waterlogged canvas of your skin,
and you will realize for the first time
that you are going to die.
that this body is a rental. a byproduct of birth.
you will sink to the bottom of the stained tub.
and cry.

three.
in the corner of a school library.
somehow it's in the library
that you will speak the loudest.
this is where you conduct a choir of poets to sing.
this is where you roll up your sleeves
and show off the accidents.
this is where the taste of guilt, lessens.

new wave [badbrain]

i am awake
and ready for war.
hands lined in blue
thoughts wrapped in glue
I AM CONTAMINATED
and i know it has arrived.
**I AM CONTAMINATED
AND GOING TO DIE**
legs surge to cross a classroom
hand sanitizer like clockwork
thoughts like a five o'clock shadow
that grows on the inside
**I AM CONTAMINATED AND
DISCONNECTED AND
NO ONE REALLY LIKES ME ANYWAY**
but i
know how to recognize you
spit no's between fixed habits
an alcoholic arguing with his booze
still pulling in, drawing out
but convinced i might be faking it
**NOTHING MATTERS AND THE
SICKNESS WILL SPREAD**
but i know how to recognize you
i can
stop you
I AM ALONE AND DISCONNECTED AND
i can
stop you
you are mine but not me
my life is
careening in pointless directions
I'M GAY AND SELFISH AND ANGRY
but i know how to recognize you
i can
stop you
GOING TO DIE

i can
CONTAMINATED
stop you
i can
POINTLESS
fight you
i can
i can't
sleep
GOING TO DIE
goodnight and
rearrangements to the same old
everything
good morning and
I AM GOING TO DIE
I AM CONTAMINATED
good morning
i am awake
and ready for war

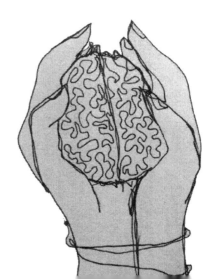

communicate

can writing
be the essence
of someone
the tendency
towards creation
i don't feel much
loyalty
to my mouth
but my hands
sing sacred

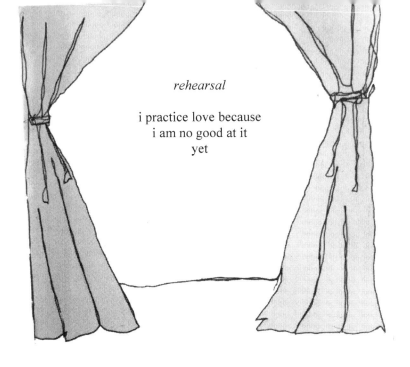

rehearsal

i practice love because
i am no good at it
yet

street lamp mirages

i drift down the street
with
feathers for fingertips
following
streetlamp mirages
and thinking about
the way you
blink
beneath the sudden
Light.

here is me

here is me,
trying to fill the empty spaces.
here is me,
selfishly scrawling myself into poetry
driving with my eyes on the mirror
crawling in circles to get here.
here is me
pulling myself across the distance
singing love to an unmet creature
i am not sure exists.
here is me, writing the easy parts
because the rest
is still bleeding

blood trial

i put my blood on trial
hired a lawyer for the parts of my mind
i don't know how to control
i assigned punishments
for the crimes committed against my body
the crimes that my body
committed against my body
sometimes i fear
the lawyers in my head
may never reach
a settlement
sometimes i fear
my body
likes it better
that way.

train, ft. fear

the answer is somewhere, i know.
i've learned to follow
graffiti arrows and folded pages –
origami fingers
pointing me onwards.
the answer is somewhere, i know.
a kindergarten memory
bleached gray from the washer
maybe
or written in the dust
of an abandoned shelf.
i wish i could meet the person
who dragged the truth through the grime
and ask them
what the hell is going on
i wonder
what the clouds would say
if i told them how scared i am
about something i'm so sure about
the truth leaves bite marks
on everything
it touches.
as a child,
i wore a hole in my throat
inhaling comfort like cigarette smoke
my journals breathed stillness
the fear of movement
now i never stop moving
but draw the same ugly flowers on every
worksheet i am handed
some habits you never leave behind.
some hopes
you never leave behind.

imagination infested

i want to be a story someday.
my imagination is infested
with thoughts of a tilted future
where to belong there?
which mess to follow?
finding my answers
means choosing my question

doubt

sometimes i'm scared
i write
because it's the only love these hands have ever known
and we're still chasing that first
taste

leftovers

i'm splayed on a hospital bed
peeled open and picked apart
a row of pulsing organs set in a row
on a stained metal tray
beside me.
already,
i miss what defines me.
empty eyes zip across time
pages fly and pencils scrape and the words buzz in my veins
and i wonder
about
the leftovers.
i'm splayed on a hospital bed
split elbows and blueberry skin
skin coiled and sliding away, stretching out to offer itself as
a new page, a final place
but i can't write anymore.
they dug in and lifted that part out of me
and now there's
nothing but
twitching organs on a metal tray and still i
i wonder
about
the leftovers
if a me without writing
is a someone who could be. but she's just
a body on a hospital bed
a red stain on a white tile
a hollowed creature peering in through my undone window
a specter
of should be

meant

someone told me in the summer
that fate is a kind of conversation.
i picture that i could
scrawl letters on bird feet
i could send a question to flight
inquire of higher places
fate could be
a promise to newcomers
a loose-looped promise
age is supposed to untie, but
i think i've let mine
strangle me
i am entangled in lifelines
of perceived purpose.
someone told me in the summer
big dreams can be a bummer
and maybe i should consider
making love a backup plan.
but how can i tell
the child living within me
that she isn't meant for this
how can i explain to my hands
all those pages have been for a back-up plan
someone told me in the winter
i could be a politician
and practice love on the weekends.
i'd work with fingers full of splinters
swallow a new crooked mission
and green vitamins
would keep me going in the mornings.
but why do i exist, if not to
write out all the backwards endings
why do i breathe
if not to push
some part of myself
back into the atmosphere
someone told me in the winter
i could thrive off a part-time passion

or crawl, cold-stomached
to follow dreams on a parkbench.
but i think it's easier
to live hungry for bread
than
to live hungry
for living.

decision

i don't know where i end
and where I begin

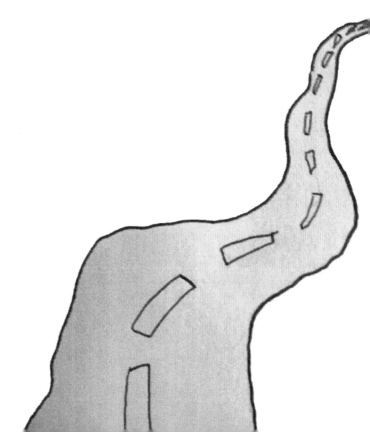

waking up

i wake up
then wait to fall asleep again.
it's been like this for a while now,
days sliding out from under
nights whispering thunder
my eyelids like to write hymns to the dark ceiling
(a fractured sort of worship.)
while my wrist bones creak, unfeeling, healing
i think
the body
never really forgets.
i'm sleeping,
seeping
into bedsheets and tiptoes
why do i rage with such luminous dread
against 3 pm's and wednesday mornings?
i'm watching time creep down elevator shafts
maybe i just need to stop listening
warp my concrete fists into open palms
it's so easy to ignore
easy to withdraw
and i've always loved to pull away.
so maybe i will.
and maybe i will
live for the dark roads
and new trees.

evergreen darkness

the parkway tried to warn us.
fog splashed over the roads
hissed under the wheels
buzzed with icy life
and broken stoplights were
bleeding caution into the windshield
but see, we were determined --
and the warnings chased us
all the way to the overlook.
on nights like this,
the mountains held roiling secrets.
pockets of toxic wonder
that vibrated under your skin.
i parked, and when my feet met the gravel,
the world smashed together.
it was that kind of darkness.
the ground pressed against the sky
up married down, left kissed right and it was
the kind of darkness that felt alive.
a darkness like heat -- the kind that breathes.
the kind that makes you feel underwater
with a gray pressure pushing into your ears.
there were no other cars
not a shred of light whispering through the fog
my own hands invisible when i
held them in front of me:
i was a flower petal
pressed between the pages of darkness.
and you, you were ethereal --
an imagined glow, but i felt you approach
heard the hesitant clank of a car door closing.
the road was gone somehow
and i didn't remember how to get home
but still i found you.
clung to you like the fog clung to us
and we stood, tall and trembling,
two evergreens lost in the fog.
it was hard to breathe through the illegal life

we'd found here.
surrounded on all edges,
you lifted your branches -- poised to float away
we were alive in isolation
but i missed silver streetlight to read you by.
still we we stood
two flickering creatures
blinking out
two evergreens
tall and trembling
sprawling branches pressed
into a page of god's notebook,
preserved evidence of aliens
sometimes,
i wonder if this really happened.

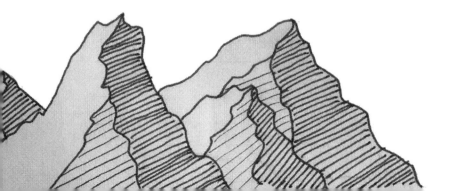

clever weather//haunted

clever weather
i trek through
oozing gray air
and hold my arms
against my stomach
as though i'm
protecting something
there. i'm followed
constantly
watched with silent
steady eyes
behind me and over
my head
i'm accustomed to
the numbness
i don't want to
channel you but
your voice is always
just right here
i think i'm haunted

classroom quality

legs crossed
hands fold, twitch,
i look around.
i hear them
mumbling
under their breath
stories translated
through gutters
and butterfly nets.
red-eyed posters
advertising lyricism,
a language
i used to speak
backwards,
i hesitate
and wonder
forwards and sideways
i do not
miss
reptilian skin
but i
guess i have to
hesitate and wonder
yesterday was all
frozen metal
my skin stuck to
skies seep into mornings
snake into afternoons
crawl into death beds
i wish my mind
knew a different place
to wander.
butterfly breath
i'm tired of talking
and tired of talking to you
hazy green eyes tilted
with a question

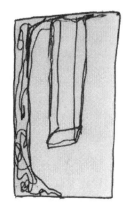

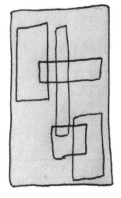

i don't ever want to answer
my accusing
ribs
still won't
forgive you
still won't
break apart and slide away
secret doors are more
than their discovery
and my bones
blockaded the doorway;
goodnight.

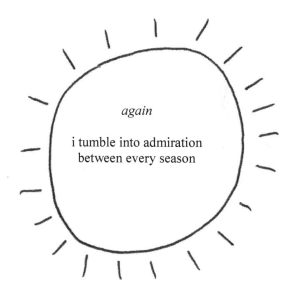

again

i tumble into admiration
between every season

come home, why don't you

smudged lavender skies
people won't take down
their christmas lights
and my father's lungs
never quite fill
'til my brother comes home

i'm sitting over water
radioactive
waiting for someone
to shake my shoulder
and tell me i'm dreaming again
i want to let my hair grow
and my feet plant roots where i walk
i want to wash my face
in baby blue and lavender
and sleep under goose bumps.

soft and solitude

keep going
hasty prayer spilt
between breath
cut my teeth
into perfect squares
hold my hands
into an equal sign
these images
never seem
to slow down
but it gets less clear
every day that i
open my eyes
it's raining
every day that i
open my eyes

absorbed

the wind makes the trees whisper here
a gust of gossip they just can't resist
as they creak and lean and hiss towards one another
selfishly,
i cannot help but feel
they are talking about me.

decode

is there something
waiting for me here
that only breathes
during the nighttime?
i love the wonder.
but it's time to keep going.
more stars are here now
airplanes blink harmonic
and i have decided
not to resent
artificial glow
the sky is always listening
what brought me here
and what is the wind trying
to tell me

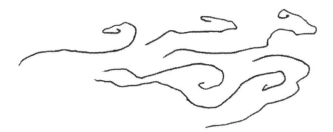

becoming

i remember
a fifth grade adventure
when fireflies
had the stars outnumbered
and i resented a boy
for launching water balloons at me
knee deep in a creek
i laughed til i fell over
and my knees burst open
spat blood, tasted iron
i slept in a tent
and wandered up a path
lit by fireflies
searching for
a bathroom.

the temperature of volume

when i'm with others,
i seem to have nothing
to say about
anything.
and when i am alone,
i have something
to say about
everything.
the silence
is such a temptress.

i thought i didn't have anything to write about

what's there to say about a cup of coffee?
fake coffee, the kind that
leaves a puddle of sugar grains at the bottom
the type honeybees
would drift towards
in the summer?
what's there to say about a crooked parking job?
wheels munching over white lines
trees laughing at the misplaced restrictions
what's there to say about a
dying movie theatre or
cigarettes crushed into snow or
shoes you feel just right in
teach me to love a perfect zero
a speed that gets you nowhere
what's there to say about static living?
standing still as to avoid leaving footprints
holding the grass like it can keep you
from falling backwards
what's there to say about spills and stains and
the pull of inner violence
when you stand at the edge of an overlook
what's there to say about a passenger seat?
pulled back and adjusted so someone's legs will fit,
but now it always sits empty
what's there to say about
churches and gas stations and flags and deathbeds?
what's there to say about a cup of coffee?

transcript from a therapy session

"it's such a vital part of myself. writing is my identity. like, hi! i'm kelsey, i write things and want to be an author when i grow up and i want to change the world. and then, there are these days where it's just so hard to get the words on the page and it feels like there's this huge vital piece of myself that i just, i can't access. and it's like, i don't even know who i am without it. writing has become a synonym for myself. what do i do when i can't? or when it's not good enough? what can i do when my life, my identity, is shaped around this thing i can't do anymore? this thing i don't want to do anymore? it's like i'm writing out of obligation to my past self. or to an audience i'm afraid of disappointing. isn't there something wrong about that?"

you caught me

i hear the clicking behind me
the dull buzz of a red recording light
where has this come from?
some white washed middle school daydream
or a funeral crowd wearing party hats?
i can shine
in the face of hypocrisy.

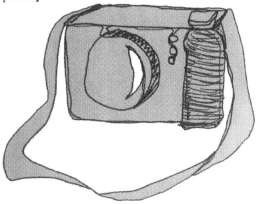

want

it's not that i want you,
or that i even really want a someone.
it's not that i want to leave,
or to stay,
not exactly.
it's not that i want to feel
or maybe it is
but i don't want to feel happy, exactly,
or sad,
or really anything in particular
it's more just that
i want.
i am devastatingly dedicated to dead-end desire.

of a previous someone: chapter one

once upon a time, there was a girl who wasn't real.
she drank wine in closets and hated her toes. she was a bad writer and a faltering reader. science sent her on a spiral. her arms and her legs were too long for her body. but her body was a cage anyway.
this unreal girl was a place of obsessions. her mind was a hard, clattering thing she didn't clean often. she only fell in love when in silence and alone, or only when it was unsafe or inconvenient. she had no interest in a sensible love. she wore a lot of black and a lot of flowers.
this was a busy, lonely girl. she had no patience and a laugh that shook buildings so they seemed to laugh with her. she almost always overreacted. her friends liked to make fun of her. mostly on the little things. but sometimes on the big things.
she worked on the weekends pushing shopping carts. when she slept, she dreamt of past boys and medicine and dying with unwrinkled hands. her soul aged backwards. as her legs grew longer her eyes grew paler. she was born thinking of her gravestone. she would die thinking of her cradle. when her parents said they loved her, she believed them. she didn't believe anyone else.
constantly, she felt herself being watched.
she felt their eyes.
and she prayed
that someday
she would wake up again.

of a previous someone: chapter two

once there was a girl born in a treasure chest.
well – not really.
she was born into a lovely casing, a shell, a vessel to fill up with her everything. this was a girl of anger. red crashing lashing gnashing rage, this was a girl of essays and explanations and silence that is hungry. she felt guilty for her treasure chest cradle and her lovely caging. she resented her unscarred elbows and ordinary eyes. she swallowed guilt pills every evening.
once, there was a girl consumed by stories. but she could only remember the boring words. everything was too familiar, words cut out by another's mouth and unfriendly to hers.
she sat in a library and dreamt of things unoriginal.

letters to god

i've been searching,
eyes reflecting phone light.
i pray to versions of you
when i drive too fast
or my body convulses into warning
i miss the certainty
that once led me.
i don't think these prayers
should hinge spineless
but i'm not sure how to reach you
anymore

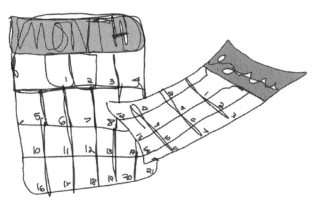

"why do we care?"

1. my blood has intentions of its own.
2. the calendar is out of breath.
3. i keep waking up when it is still dark out.
4. homeless doorframes hope for a heartbeat.
5. i tied balloons to my ribcage to try and make myself feel
just
       a little
              lighter.
6. someday, someday, i will dream again.

langue

peut-être si j'explique
dans une langue different
je peux découvrir
pourquoi je suis comme ça.
peut-être si je pense
de ton visage quand je réveille
mes rêves serait différent –
plus...grand, en quelque sorte
plus optimiste

{maybe if i explain
in a different language
i can discover
why i am like this.
maybe if i think
of your face when i wake up
my dreams will be different –
more...big, somehow
more optimistic}

three skeletons i have loved, and why

one.
the shaking bones of my shelter. a home where we taught flowers to grow.
when i was young, my father told me i had a green thumb but he had green hands. and i was made of branches.
our house was a mess, a whimsical nest of rest,
it is a place i wait to return to.

two.
i have loved the skeleton of a raven.
the outline of a someone.
i have traced the edges of this love because i know it is hollow;
that is the only way it can fly.
who was i,
to fill a raven's hollow bones with honey.
who was i,
to love the way you rebuilt me.

three.
this body still feels new to me. these flightless bones waterlogged,
these eyes unripe and unreal.
i am built around a skeleton.
flesh and skin and branches.
i am evolution's experiment.
i am, becoming.

here: an experiment in being

i am going to conduct an experiment.
i am going to park the car
and lean the seat back
and stare at the glossy wrinkled light switch
on the ceiling –
the one that drains the car battery
if you leave it on overnight.
i am going to stretch my legs
and let my toes scratch an itch on the brake pedal.
i am going to let my fingers hum along
the stained sides of the driver's seat.
i am going to look at the brown splotch on the ceiling,
next to that glossy wrinkled light switch.
i am not going to wonder how it got there.
i am not going to think about statistics homework.
or the tune that death whistles when he's bored.
i am not going to think about leaving.
not this town, this country, or this body.
i am not going to think about what i'll do
when tomorrow takes its first breath.
i am going to conduct an experiment.
here.
lying flat on my back in this laid-down car seat,
staring at the glossy wrinkled light switch on the ceiling.
i am going to rehearse breathing.
conversion.
oxygen to energy.
sun to sugar.
i am going to focus on the hereness. here.
i am going to focus on the nowness. now.
i am going to burn in an ear-eating eavesdrop
i am going to listen to the howl of this stained silenced skin
i am going to fill my mouth with my knuckles and listen
to what crawls out between the cracks
i am going to conduct an experiment.

17

i have no patience for a soft sort of heat.
for the kind of ending
that hesitates

Chapter Four: Growing Forwards

this is where we leave.
in a new direction.
welcome
and please
keep looking

"enter, as particles of light, through fissures in my skin.
grow, as all things must in the dark:
fed by the dreams of the day."
—brie cunliffe

i wear seatbelts now

i wear seatbelts
now
in search of better days,
i gaze into now
i am a terror to untruth.
i am a terror to unlove.
i wear seatbelts
now
i flipped the phrase
"just in case"
to mean striving
for survival

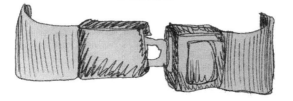

multiply

after the crash
all was a freezing handrail
all was an unspent weekend
all was the end and emptiness of something.
there is no way to make amends for this behavior.
is it selfish,
to wish to be a thousand versions of myself?
to imagine
separating and unpeeling,
letting each layer grow into something new?
after the crash
i was built anew

light trick

watch!
clever tricks played by gravity
i'm soarin' over a memory
wait!
the moon hangin' on a fish hook
wait, hey watch, look!
solar eyes
moondust cheekbones
the sky a wrinkled film of skin
stretchin' over us
how
can the moon outshine the sun
when it's just usin' the sun's light
to begin with
are
reflections
always brighter?
unpeel eyelids
i catch a glimpse
of the moon reflected in your sunglasses
everything's more beautiful
when it's reflected in your sunglasses
the moon, a button sewed into the sky
a secret sewed between your lips
dodge
eye contact with skylit reflections
and well meaning camera lenses
shifting reflections
orbiting eyes
watch!

an ode to andrew

my pen has long neglected you the attention you deserve
and i think that's because of the way you
let the love roll right off you –
that's the way you do these things.
but i
like the way you hold your silverware
and kiss her like a quick and gentle habit.
i like your steady stance
indifferent and nonchalant, just
letting life just have its way with you
always on the right side of the sky
i like the way you talk when it means something
and the subtle silence when it doesn't
i like the way you move, like your feet
already know where they're going – and they don't
need your permission.
they always take such good care of you.
i like the way you lay, warm and safe,
a place to rely on and retreat to.
i like sharing
blankets and windows and hash browns and mishaps
with you
i like your shrug and the shape of your hands
and when you say to me
"you've got it"
in that casual way that claims there's no doubt about it.
i like that you cut your hair
and let me change clothes in your car
and tell me when i look good.
i like your presence, i like your style and
affinity for late nights.
i like how you rub my back when we hug,
like your fingers are pressing kisses to my shoulder blades.
i like that we can belong to each other
in a way that lacks romance.
i like that you don't bullshit, i like that you

keep me honest, keep me hopeful, that you can bring out
all my best bits and pieces.
i just like you, i guess.
i like you a lot.

colorado

i like the air here
it has such strange
personality

attention
    ft. trying

i don't listen.
but they talk anyway.
i'm driving
in a box of blue curtains
CRASH THE CAR
hands careful
on a glass steering wheel
CRASH THE CAR
i don't listen
but they talk anyway.
CRASH THE CAR
PINCH YOUR WRISTS
YOU'RE NOT IN CONTROL
i ease on the brakes
and turn the corner.
CRASH THE CAR
THESE HANDS AREN'T YOURS
i forgot where i was going
because i forgot you were
in the car with me
CRASH THE
and you're dancing, head bopping,
giant goofy smile
there are trees out the window
IT'S ALL ENDING ANYWAY
PINCH YOUR WRISTS
MAKE SURE YOU'RE AWAKE
i'm driving you home
your hair smells like oranges
CRASH THE CAR
i park outside your house
and we kiss without undoing our seatbelts
IT'S ALL ENDING ANYWAY
your butterfly-net hands

scoop my knuckles up
HE'S GOING TO DIE SOMEDAY
your mouth unravels
and i surface from myself enough to
understand what you're asking
WHY ARE YOU EVEN TRYING
YOU'RE GOING TO DIE TOO
SOMEDAY YOU'RE GOING TO LISTEN TO US
"yeah," i say
my hand convulses in my lap
"i'm okay."
fingernails to wrist bone
i spit blood at the feet of obedience
i don't listen
but they talk anyway
your eyes follow my hands
wherever they go
YOU'RE GOING TO HURT HIM
you unbuckle your seatbelt
your house glows soft orange out the window
i unbuckle mine
and when i look at you
i know
you know already
HE'S GOING TO HURT YOU
so i try to pull the filth out from my throat
hair and bugs and hand sanitizer
retch it into my palms
and reach out to show you
WHY ARE YOU EVEN TRYING
you smile.
my lungs open from closed fists
and flatten into welcome mats.
HE DOESN'T CARE ABOUT YOU
we talk in the car for two hours
your hair smells like oranges
the windows are tense and frost grows there
your hand
plants daisies behind my ears
sprinkles paper snowflakes over my shoulders

you leave
and i am left with
a garden of giggles blooming in my mouth
i start the engine
pull myself out of park
and start the drive home
CRASH THE CAR
i don't listen.
but they talk anyway.

simple

somewhere
the flowers sway smiling in blood-caked soil.
hands vibrate over fractured foreheads,
throats split with thirst but
the only water these people have
collects in their armpits.
sleep is a snitch, an endless itch
travel a gamble to save someone.
to help
we build fences
and lock airports.
see, we are far too busy
floating upside down in satin sheets
lungs heaving velvet water
backbones bleached from too much time
at the swimming pools
to notice
such simple suffering

the night before leaving

we were but
dim jagged outlines
that night:
uneven pieces of the sky
that had come loose.
the moon clung to a handkerchief
and dabbed nostalgia out of her eyes,
watching us and following us
with her home light.
how precious,
these moments before
the first step away.

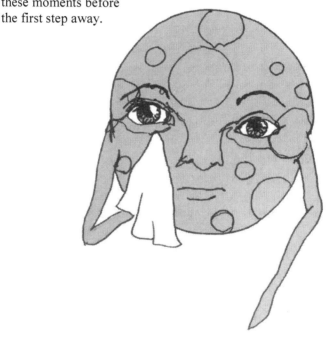

fourteen days

we spend these days wandering.
we imagine signing our names on white skies
memorizing the curving rims of cold cups
reading to each other with the engine running.
we spend these days wondering.
pushing boundaries and challenging heartbeats
we argue with safety even when
it shows us danger's teeth.
i want to give every part of myself to this.
these explosive boiling non-stop days
i have to go
i'm counting down but never stop moving
and i love her
for the way she draws when i share myself
the way her eyes shift in the presence of poetry
and i love him
for his grounded tolerance of volume
and his knees nestled around a blanket
and i love her, too –
for her unapologetic outrage
and her,
for her presence that always invites confession
and her,
for the way she refuses to fear honesty.
these have been days dream-washed and fearful
honest and clueless
extraordinary and alive
days of dancing and screaming and driving and smiling
days of close-calls and electricity, edges and outlines
insides and outsides, sweat and pink and pavement
forgiveness and forgetfulness
my two week summer
smiles
without fear
of the endings

quiet

it's a soft space all of a sudden.
dark and lukewarm --
a tight tense moment of breathlessness.
my mind
has gone quiet.
i didn't know it could be like this.
marble hands and frozen lungs,
even my blood stills
to notice.
my mind
has gone quiet.
it's a fragile quiet,
frail and quivering quiet
a downdraft before splitting open
could i breathe into sweet silence
before the skin breaks?
i pray into
the cracks in sidewalks
that the quiet isn't here to hurt me
i pray into
the musty kiss of tree trunks
that the hollow won't haunt me.
my mind
has gone quiet.
perhaps now
there is room enough
for both of us

mai lai: summer solstice

strange
i can write in silence here, in public places.
these people are
singing of honey dew and hunger
voices foreign to violence
and strangers
spill apologies between novocain teeth
squeeze screams from knotted lungs
and i am just here to write and to love and to listen
and yes, we are terrible.
and yes, i come from this.
and yes, i am a part of this.
it is the longest day of the year.
strange

winning

clever chaos,
this is never not the place for
unlocked thoughts
scratched elbows and
bright unlikely places.
this is the place
war fought for.
this is the place
we celebrate coffins.
it was supposed to feel
like winning

sonder

emerald circle sunglasses
and socks pulled halfway up hairy calves
he stops
fidgeting with his backpack strap.

"what building is this?"

an airplane growls overhead.
the air is marble smooth
and smells like heat
like electricity and burnt out matches.

a mailman trudges behind him
tugging a cart of packages down the road
clanking, scraping, gravel aching
no one looks his way.

"no, i mean – like, what do they teach here?"

behind the mailman
a mother stands with her son
from a distance
her smile tight like a violin string
tense and out of tune.
she grimaces as she leans to hand her son the phone.

"i'm doing, uh, i'm doing – a tour here?"

a stranger sits with headphones on
their fingers taste
the grainy edge
of a park bench

"i was just wondering if you knew."

the reflections shift

in his emerald circle sunglasses
green waters churning.
wave goodbye

"thanks."

what we've done

there is something in the southern sky.
the things we know
trickling dark
bugs that bite
counts to three.
one. two. three.
what it takes to stand, and to listen.
to turn away.
there is something in the southern sky.
something terrible.
a reminder.
blinking body parts.
an inheritance.
a nightmare.
there is something in the southern sky.

i was so scared to speak

she breathes with her eyes.
those eyes, a queer dear magic fear
asking me a question.
she speaks with her eyes.
words tumble between her eyelashes
her mouth is silent but those eyes are loud
lord, those eyes...are loud.
what kind of song are they missing?
what kind of birds like to live there?
and i wonder,
what she thinks of
the rain

muchness in the missing

so much depends upon
an appreciation of your own freckles.
tracing lines between birthmarks
naming skin spaces after constellations
so much depends upon
the smiles we share in the hallway.
brief eyes slipping beneath footsteps
a flicker and a flashlight:
an establishment of space and closeness.
so much depends upon this,
this immersive starvation.
this expanding ache for knowledge
this missing of mountains and oceans
this distance from our hometowns.
so much depends upon
the trees here…
and the roots
we miss

ways to live

you are alive.
everyone else is an expression of yourself. so take care of yourself and take care of others unless it takes away from the care you need for yourself. seek pleasure and comfort. see what is wrong with the world and trust your emotions to move you to action. follow what makes you feel things. find and see the beauty in everything. getting excited over something small is wonderful. crying is okay. crying in front of others is okay. laughing is okay. laughing without others is okay. it's okay. trust yourself. love yourself. love the world, in all its brokenness. because
you are alive.
that is a phenomenon.

happy-ings

i could pick apart these happenings
push them into unhappenings and rehappenings,
a backwards glimpse of happy-ings.
the unease born from this will not be wasted.
i promise this.
your grim untucked lips remind me of my mountains.

she

she crosses the sky
a zigzag timeline
of sacred light.
she puffs soft into the embers
cradled in the cracks between fingers
a fire born of
sky skin and cloudscrapers
she flames the poet's pen
she rises
in the nighttime.

mo[u]rning time

who knows
how to begin something like this?
here i am
swallowing pills of forgiveness
waiting for the sharp shards
to loosen in my skin
waiting for my muscles to let go
and relax
sitting cold on a metal park bench
wishing i'd decided
to wear shoes for once.
the edge of the sky knows
only one direction
and though i'm sat
facing east
all the clouds seem
to cover me
if the sun is rising
i can only feel it bleed.
and these things
are written about too often
but i swear i can't breathe
through the sunflowers
growing in my throat
they reach for light
climbing between my teeth
it's no fun to kiss
in the springtime.
how lovely
to find company
in abandoned playgrounds
and half-filled park benches
how foolish and how strange
to let your eyes bubble over
when the birds
and the aliens

are watching

what wishful woes to worship

where do we go from here?
feet singing sore from the gravel
sharpies in my pocket
a spineless sunflower buried
between these pages.
i make it a goal
to spend some time
in the company of something above me
i swear they listen
but they never speak back.
where do we go from here?
i could use my feet as a compass
rotate in randomness
trust toes and ankles
to pick a place to wander.
how many people
will learn to unlove me?
everywhere i go
is there someone making a bargain
with early evenings and lovesick mornings
spinning a deal
with a grandfather clock
pressing lip and tongue against the red mouth
of a fire alarm
i have to ask
is love a prerequisite for losing?
what silly things
i have selected to serenade
what wishful woes to worship.
i just wish i had
some sort of
direction

up

stationed above
no one can see me
from here.
the lake pulls against us,
shaky ruffles arcing against wind,
soft spoken laughter
lighting down the spine
of this mountain bed
i am wonderment
in the presence of this.
a forest of green
cold and clear awayness
my tongue rests
with nothing to say.
let's stay.

co. mtns

the grass swings
in broken half-orbit
and trees wink
with black pupils.
wild flowers hold
no apology here.
every second in unusual light
is something to kneel to.
the wind winds music
and tapestries through
the seeing trees.
the path putters earthly guidance
branches, knobbed knuckles,
clenched against coming coldness.
it's so hard to grow here.
but we do it
anyway.

de-me'ing

am i here? i think
i'd like to be –
sitting somewhere near the ceiling
arching blue
and dreaming.
nothing's real
until i write it.
over as soon as
i find it.
i've felt
eyes following my feet,
the earth sighing as i leave
i've felt buildings tense
as i approached them
what can this mean
but i'm real-ing?
is that the word?
the action of reality.
the verb of vitality,
the doing of being.
what can this mean
but i'm seeing? something,
somewhere, maybe not here but
this i can say with sensitivity
in some way,
i am here.
and in some way,
i am supposed to be.

interview

my mother's mother
wore a nametag of day
a maiden name like a reminder
that the light is yet to come.
she comes from
cold glasses stuck to sweaty palms
reaching across a fence
with shouts over her shoulder
she comes from
a roadside teacher
whispering
of a new pattern
a cat named jeremiah
who she loved because
he always got into trouble
but always
came
home

man's hands

don't break me down
into your favorite sexy segments
i am not a too-tall building
waiting for reconstruction
i have no need of a man's hands.
your callused palms have no business
drawing diagrams of
something like me
i don't adhere
to messy manly measurement
i have no itch between my thighs
that sings for a new builder.
gardens will grow whether or not
you criticize the shape of the flowers
the length of the roots
the time it spends growing.
keep your hands away from me.
i am not
a construction site
i am not a place to be rebuilt by
someone else's hands
i turn light into sugar
and grow fine on my own.
i am peeking out of the soil now
i am reaching claws and branches
to new blue spaces
i can grow through concrete
taste the underside of so many shoes
crushed down and rearranged
but i just
keep
coming
back again.
i have no need of a man's hands.

this, of us

i wish i could take that moment and paint it onto my walls.
swipe the colors across my ceiling so when
i wake up on cold mornings i look up and remember
why i wait out the winter.

recipe

defying statistics
i'm lovin' it
selfish hypocrite
i'm lovin' it
i made it back safe – don't worry.
existence chose me
and i'm lovin' it

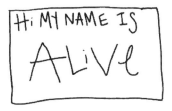

light-sick in america

light-sick in america, i am
swept up in the arms of a clown
look up and
uncle sam's makeup is cracked
into white desert drought
his lipstick crawls across
the underside of a jutted chin

light-sick in america
we're locking kids in jail cells
but don't mind since
at least the product sells

light-sick in america
we will unlearn how to learn here
unlearn how to leave, unlearn how to love
in blueprint buildings
designed for criminals
we'll sit tied to a desk
scores sliced into our necks

light-sick in america
we ink in silence and rest
forget about the rest
right hand on my chest

light sick in america
watch the news like an
experiment in unbeing and
rebecoming
laughter bubbles out our lips
in hazy patriot light
sick in america!

i'm a bug smashed into the windshield

so my guts smear red, white, and blue!
i'll undo my body!
fold myself like a flag,
into a perfect traditional triangle --
i'll squeeze all my pieces into an envelope
and mail it to the white house
since they say it's not mine anymore!

light-sick in america!
i think
these nuclear weapons
have been held too close to the
flesh of this nation
i think
the radiation must be
undoing and rearranging the
sequence of our dna
growing cancerous laughter
into the skin, the tongue, the brain of this nation
i think
we can't have much longer now,
in the light,
sick in america.

our light's sick
in america.

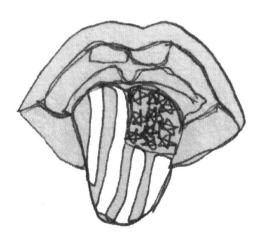

slip

she told me yesterday
there is a section of self
i refuse to offer.
strange, i thought,
as my veins are propped open
and my tables bend
under the weight of confession
she nudged my secrets with her toe,
lifted her eyebrow into a question
and i smiled
just like i practiced.
"what a beautiful mind,
to imagine there must
be more to me."
i could live
in the slimy silence
that follows a compliment.
she relaxed
allowed a narrow smile,
her eyebrows back to earth.
i should be more careful.
untuck the bent pages, let no red edges
stick out
so no one gets the idea
to tug on some old section of myself.
there is still so much
that i can't let leave here.
i'm not sure
what colors would crush me
if these thoughts touched oxygen

i wonder what she would say
at the sight of
that

terms and conditions

in terms of forgiveness,
i'm making small progress.
it seems i am still
growing out from
under you, i don't like
that i have the same lips that
touched you, i think i'm
still in a lilac dark-space.
in terms of anger
i'm making some progress.
i've cooled from
red to green to something like blue
but i've always associated blue
with you so i stripped that too
and now i am nothing but warm color.
yes, i've rejected numbness.
yes, i've learned to love being forgotten.
in terms of sadness
i have abandoned the default
and am hoping the battery doesn't run out
i'm busy here, i am running so fast
the sad is out of breath
and i think
i like it
that way.

narcissist

this perception of vitality
is somewhere between foolish and selfish
why should i expect my name to appear
in your bedtime conversation
why should i assume
any degree of mattering
when it comes to you
i could
rat out the clocks
embarrass the summertime
call out the wind and the sunshine
but how could i expect
my name to abduct your newfound wonder
how could i expect
the thought of me to fill your mouth
with sweaty watermelon and sickly dust
i only hope
you are learning the laws of attention
and
though maybe the letters of my name
never giggle against your eardrums
i hope my
wrists reach down the throat of your dreams
just to pull some suffering
out of you

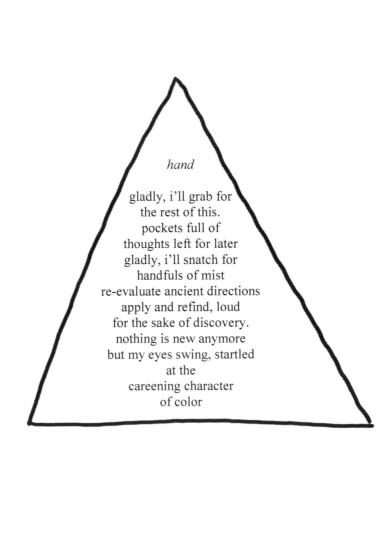

hand

gladly, i'll grab for
the rest of this.
pockets full of
thoughts left for later
gladly, i'll snatch for
handfuls of mist
re-evaluate ancient directions
apply and refind, loud
for the sake of discovery.
nothing is new anymore
but my eyes swing, startled
at the
careening character
of color

what it carries

ouch.
here, i can see the
open and close of the
overworld
like heaven's caught on the hinges
the clouds shift like gears
click-click-click and
ouch.
i don't think
the ground expected to have
so much to carry
step on a crack
that's a break in its back
the spine of this earth
is heaving
is splintering
is crackling
under the weight
ouch.
i'll conduct oil puddles to sing.
they'll glimmer treeline reflections
birdsong abductions,
i'll watch as all the
earth-eating footprints
fill with gasoline.
and we, too,
will hollow
just to fill up
with giggling cigarette eulogies.
ouch.
but would a no trespassing sign
help

calling all loveless lovers

calling all loveless lovers!
i have a treat for you.
a silly similiar someone
who can rip your eyes wide open.
look my way before i slip away
because believe me,
you won't want to miss this.
i...am a bird call cutting across
lavender wind.
i am a lonesome linear lime-taste love
and i will chase away *all* the bitter
dating a poet is good for the soul
and bad for your health but
hey!
calling all loveless lovers!
i am such a sucker for all the things
i haven't seen!
i have come from bruised thighs
and colonist hands
text message marriages
in the absence of "and"s
write me a word that'll hook
our names together
don't listen to my loveless lovers
i was good to them and
they were bad at me, see
i come from blue and red lovers
i come from too loud, too touched
then solitary confinement
i've got a kink for unbalance, babe
but kindness really turns me on
so
calling all loveless lovers!
why not give me a try?

step

unbutton memories
under undone light
night crinkling
in the corners of your eyes
passing blood through earbuds
a vein we share.

he

in the heavens
he has pitched a tent for the sun.
what glistening shelter, riskful wreckage;
nothing is hidden from its heat.
i beg
between crackling teeth,
across copperhead tongue:
forgive me my hidden faults, for
who can discern his errors
and it is so easy
to lust for lasting.
it's the way
his hands
have pressed me

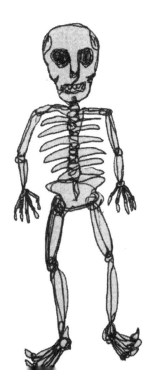

cleanse

there are no lightbulbs here,
no shadows over tennis shoes.
i stand at the fountain and
let the sacred beads sink into the water
dip my hands into the ageless chemicals
and watch
waves of yellow seep out my wrists.
i press water droplets to my waist line,
designs to carry with me
since pens aren't allowed here
and if if I stop to listen
home echoes
out the window

skin pockets

i wonder if i could clear my head of this.
zip my skin into pockets
and duck inside
translate ashen autumn
into a new, bluer
pace

a list of things to think about

1. sapphire sunlight, walking in darkness as spring breathes around me
2. empty hours
3. ruinous time-zones
4. soft mint mornings
5. linear progression and understanding with my eyes closed
6. scraped knees
7. cold water
8. blurred windows and white knuckles
9. sharpened pencils
10. warm places
11. hoodies that cling to the breath of a campfire
12. glinting game cards
13. sitting cross-legged in the dark
14. dusty wood floors
15. the moment right before the end, right in that sugar sweet metallic moment when for just an instant
                                         time
                    holds
                                      its breath.

 *morning*

you ripped your fingers
pulling apart
a vortex
you tore
the churning
whirlpool
crushed it between
the pages of your journal
then spread it
over toast
and munched on the past
on your
cold
walk
to work.

reasons to rise

what if
i drew a map of the world across my kneecaps
so every time i fall
i know i must rise
to lift the world
out of the dust

well

my mind
has no
friends

pray

there's a lavender lip secret
brushing over soft places
snow angels writhing in sleek thunder –
they figured it out early on.
that
you are not
evergreen lovesick clarity
you are not
tuesdays and chai sweetness
you are not
the place i kneel.
you are familiar.
but an escapee
does not pray
to come home

dear december 6th

what slender grief
peeled you open
today
and why do you
leave puddles by
roadsides
i suppose
you are tired
a steel gray face
leaking sorrow
in wait of some
tomorrow
you won't get to see.
well,
i won't lie
i'm waiting
for you to die
for your cloud-stirred
thievery
to recede
and live
somewhere
between my shoulder blades
a place you are
familiar with.
so just
give me some time,
december 6th,
and cheer up soon;
i'll be waiting for you,
and i hope
i'll see you
again

lust is not a sin lust is not a sin lust is not a sin

the priest called it
a distortion of love
this wild and ruthless feeling
like the world just wasn't big enough.
like there weren't enough lips to taste
hands to touch
shoulders to bump against.
he said lust
was an unsteady place to grow from
a spot too shallow to hold roots
but i think
you don't need depth to linger in
temporary healing
and besides,
an argument based on ownership
is not an argument at all.
the priest called it
one of god's great gifts
(was that sex or my body?)
and great gifts must be used carefully
dangerously, cautiously
in a way so as not to shame the giver
because, after all, we live in god's body
and anything we do to and with it
must be a reflection of him
i don't think that's true
i think god loves us enough to give us a little privacy
i don't think he gave me a body just so
i could be ashamed of it
and i don't think he'll condemn me
for the feelings i get from it.
i guess what i'm saying is,
yes i believe there's more
than the wanting flesh
and wires in the brain

and bone and knuckle under my skin
i believe this body is a vessel for

something greater
but i don't believe in mistrusting
the things this body whispers to me.
i think maybe the body
is god's way of speaking to us
and if both people are willing
maybe there's no shame in
attacking
the lonely. and
maybe god
understands us enough
to smile and
glance the other way.

an ode to molly

she's wrapped in a blueberry sleeping bag
tossing honey cut phrases my way
she's direct
and likes to speak her mind.
we've spent today
facing spring's teeth
(rain jackets are just never enough.)
we ate beans out of cups
and rode a green bus
to places i'd be afraid to go alone
in 18 years, 11 months, 8 hours
i could return here
and re-find a someone's eclipse
and until then
i'll be waiting

older now//playground

this is an afternoon of
strawberry tops
and sore throats
trees bouncing flavor, stretching
into the sunlight.
there's a way about the dirt spots
dusty loops, caverns of truth-like earth
peeking out like bald spots.
a man tumbles over the hill
laughter exploding as his dog
races after
there's something about the jungle gym
i could never sit and write
when i was young enough to flip myself
around the bars
but now i sit and write
because i am young enough to see
how much there is to say.

summer hymn

militant wrists
and sun-fried braids down backbones –
we are being watched.
sneakers crush chalk into august pavement
windmills always in a hurry –
we are being caught.
go.

higher grounds

steam leaps, unravels
stretching to seep warmth
into colder times:
a promise
rising from the rim
of a coffee cup.
this seems to be a place
people return to.
a safe place
where the door stays open
to invite the light
in.
a place
to go
when in search of
higher grounds.

look out

fire alarms unravel into bloodstreams
uncover and unpull
we're crafting a new character
laughing in the face of truth
baiting
and
waiting.

something like my somewhere, part i

i wish i could keep this place
there's a trust invested in these mountains
we crawl across the edges and
sleep into the unsafety
we like to live on the verge of balance
and the mountains
like to hold us
as the wind practices
summer

something like my somewhere, part ii

the mountains bump shoulders
and wrap their arms around me
hug of home
i still fall backwards but
what a rare gift,
to sit soft in the presence of god.

to do list

punctuate your posture with purpose
sun-fried sustainability dripping down your neck
honey ringtones and clever miscommunications.
practice artistry in your greetings
practice trust in your goodbyes
follow the threads that make up your sweater
and pretend you wanna get better
because that's the way it's gonna go
here.
follow my failing fantasies.
this maniac mischief has no need
for self-hatred;
doubt
is not a prerequisite
for kindness

spring awakening

it's finally warm again
canopies shimmering heat waves
i've missed spring's kiss
north carolina is a floral sort of belonging
the song of the evergreens
and mismatched pajamas
the trees keep
trying to touch
the soft
blue
ceiling

green mtn

i've missed walking barefoot
and the mountains have missed my skin
steady father warm and green
bring me loving rain
while i leave dents in cars and
chase things that fly;
i know these words don't align
in a way that dances, matches
but still
they are mine
and there is something
breathless
about that

rabbit

it's a sick trick
in my corrupted blood
something like submission
something like silence.
i could court the holy water
arm the elements to
fight back against god's orders
but instead i
sit still
back straight
two feet on the ground
and allow obedience.
it's a sick trick
in my corrupted blood
this aversion to volume
the dragging rotation of decision
these secret feet, scared of lifting.
i'll put the law to a firing squad
turn sleep into water
and boil out all the orders
bubbles of obedience
snapping into steam -- no.
instead i
sit still
back straight
and allow obedience.
that's just what i am.
that's just the ache
that nature takes.
what am i, but a rabbit
cowering in camouflage
it's a sick trick
in my corrupted blood.

gas-pedal pillows

what a catastrophic comedy
this back and forth
and dulled affection.
it's too late to repent.
the rain is here
it forgets how to hesitate
maybe keeping
is political
maybe keeping
is safe
but choice is the rarest part
and i don't want to practice
choosing preservation
when i've been asleep on
gas-pedal pillows

honey

milky porcelain woman
sitting behind a name plate
when i raise my hand
my shoulder scrapes chalky joints
blink over empty eyes
what a pretty girl
what sugar pale lips
what soft spun skin
hush down, honey
a porcelain woman
shouldn't chew
a mouthful of thumbtacks
a voice so loud has no business
in such a royal mouth
when i lower my hand
hollow skin scrapes together again
swallow the thumbtacks
and squeeze honey from
between the cracks in my teeth
milky porcelain woman
drizzling sweetness
all
over
the tablecloth

i visit this place in hopes of healing

i find god in unfelt places
stretching greens that hold my feet
and arcing blues that lift my arms
i want to lean into this mountain
like i lean into a steady shoulder
i want to feel
and let it feel me
i want to take
and let it take me.
but the trees still
don't speak my language

language

i'm trying to decide
what language best fits in my mouth
whether my tongue
turns best along
the ridges of riot
or slips soft along
the slopes of silent
no phrase flips fluent
along my lips now
i suppose
i've got to choose one
first

holly's taking pictures again

my friend disappeared,
fascinated by fields and falling fences.
i'm somewhere
2,870 miles above the ocean
and i think she's gone off somewhere
to take pictures.
cars slow down, ease in my direction
but no one puts in park
my legs are sprawled on pavement
cradling a journal
while my friend is transfixed somewhere,
perhaps expecting me to follow.
the bugs don't bite here,
when i stay out of the grass.
people like to look in my direction
when their engines funnel past.
i'm numbering the afternoons
til i go away again.
i crave screens and sleep and outerspace
but instead i am writing
in a vein of god's wrist
he likes to keep me here

3:30

i drive people places when
it's raining and they want
to kiss in secret and
buy black coffee when it's
a white-shout sky out
i've been waiting in the parking lot
for half an hour
my teeth hurt but
i'm unhungry;
nothing tastes good anymore.
there's no space
large enough
to be worth crossing
no solution
far away enough
to be worth considering
i can't waste sweat
on a half-way escape.
instead
i wear sweaters
and let my teeth
shift and settle
into anxious agreement.
apply too many adjectives
to this
maybe i can
catch this feeling
and load it into a label
maybe
it'll be easier
then

i found god in a green light

i found the garden of eden today.
i found it in a greenlight.
it shrieked through the windshield
and fell into my lap
i found the garden of eden today.
it vibrated sin and wonder
a pool of lime, a forest swaying over kneecaps
while the engine hummed hymns
beneath me.
every conversation is a bite into prayer
teeth into confession
jaw breaking hell into pieces
easier to chew.
i found the garden of eden today.

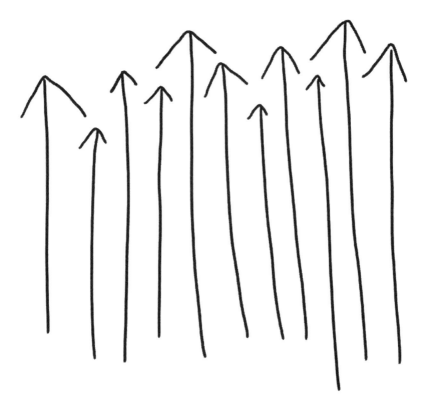

the last twelve hours

the smoke slings in our faces
stings our noses, gathers under our eyelids,
churns and swirls, crests and breaks
we stayed warm but didn't sleep well
we grind charcoal into journals
share breath with the embers
autumn is a certain sort of closeness.
the leaves crinkle
a paper carpet of color
and i've never much liked autumn before
but
there is healing
in the falling

remote

all last night i dreamt of this morning.
most people talk about the past
because it is over.
i talk about the past
because it is
still
happening

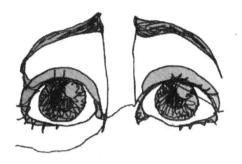

time travel

will i abandon this too?
i wonder if somewhere,
an older me is trying to move
backwards to find myself
here again
i wonder if somewhere
i am always searching
crawling backwards and forwards in time
always reaching
for the forgotten colors
of yesterday